SURE SUCCESS IN ORAL ENGLISH
Copywright © Onye kingsley 2014

All Rights Reserved

ISBN 978-0-9569415-6-5

First Published 2014 by
KINGSLEY PUBLISHERS (UK) LTD.
76 Foxcombe Fieldway Addington Village
Cr0 9ez,
Croydon
London.
www.kingsleybooks.co.uk

Printed for KINGSLEY PUBLISHERS.

SURE SUCCESS

IN

ORAL ENGLISH LANGUAGE FOR EVERYONE

(ADDITIONAL READING MATERIAL FOR NEW LEARNERS)

Onye Kingsley N.

(BA:ED, MA ENGLISH)

1

DEDICATED TO MY PARENTS

LATE CHIEF TONY & MARTINA ONYE FOR THEIR CONSTANT SUPPORT AND LOVE.

TABLE OF CONTENT

PREFACE

The idea of this work is borne out of the need to mount a timely exam-rescue operation for candidates who are preparing for any Level in English Language Examinations.

Experience has shown, that only, infinitesimal percentage of the total number of our students perform creditably well, in their GSCE,/A.LEVEL English Language Examinations nation-wide.

This unpleasant development is a nightmare to the author's dream world, hence his humble and determined effort to embark on this work, to once and for all bring our strayed scholars back into the path of Sure Success in their various English Language Examinations.

A perusal, of the book will clearly illuminate your mind with the clear and noble intentions of the author.

-Onye Kingsley N.

FORWARD

Success is always a winner. Hard work is always greatly rewarded. This book is unique in confronting the problems of students in English Language examinations.

A new approach to the learning process to pass GCSE /A LEVEL examinations at the first sitting is well presented. It is an inevitable companion for all school leavers in competitive examinations, for which the book is precisely designed. Always remember that nothing succeeds like success.

SRA MACAULAY PhD Birmingham

SENIOR LECTURER,

O.A.U. IFE.

"SURE SUCCESS" IN ORAL ENGLISH LANGUAGE

ORGANS OF SPEECH

ENGLISH VOWELS, CONSONANTS AND DIPHTONGS.

ALL THESE ARE ARTICULATED THROUGH THE HELP OF THE ORGANS OF SPEECH (MOUTH)."

INTRODUCTION TO ORAL ENGLISH

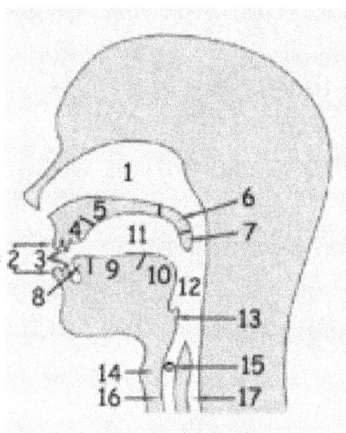

The Organs of Speech

1 - nasal cavity
2 - lips
3 - teeth
4 - aveolar ridge
5 - hard palate
6 - velum (soft palate)
7 - uvula
8 - apex (tip) of tongue
9 - blade (front) of tongue
10 - dorsum (back) of tongue
11 - oral cavity
12 - pharynx
13 - epiglottis
14 - larynx
15 - vocal cords
16 - trachea
17 - esophagus

The above diagram refers to speech organs, they are basically used in articulating the speech process.

The originator of the speech is the lungs, the muscles that support the lungs from lungs to Trachea (windpipe). It is the air that comes from the lungs that we use in speech, the muscle presses the lungs and speech is produced, so the starting point of all speech is the lungs.

The throat also help in speech production in men, it is larger than in women, the bounds of flesh in the throat we call the VOCAL CORD (Adams apple).

The area above the throat is significant for speech making usually the mouth and the nose. When the nose is closed, the mouth produces ORAL SOUNDS, when the mouth is closed and the sounds come from the nose, these are referred to as NASAL SOUNDS.

(i)   Sounds from the mouth – ORAL SOUNDS

(ii)   Sounds from the nose – NASAL SOUNDS

Nevertheless, it is possible to have sounds from both the mouth and nose at the same time.

The lips – these are organs of speech, we have the upper lip and the lower lip, immediately behind the lips we have the teeth, upper teeth and lower teeth, then the upper mouth and lower mouth, upper floor and lower floor of the mouth.

Immediately after the upper teeth there is a raised portion, continued from one point to another. This is referred to as the ALVEOLAR RIDGE, then we have the HARD PALATE, and after that we have the SOFT PALATE, which terminates with a fleshy tail like thing called UVULA.

NOTE: A tape recorder is usually used for the listening comprehension.

CLUES TO THE TACKLING OF LISTENING COMPREHENSION

PREAMBLE ON ORGANS OF SPEECH

For any meaningful attempt on oral English, a copious emphasis must first be placed on the study of organs of speech, without which the study of oral English will be null and void.

Firstly, it should be noted that organs of speech (mouth) includes the following: the lungs, the vocal cords, the velum, hard palate, alveolar ridge, teeth, lips and the tongue – all these are organs of speech.

The process of speech production starts from the lungs which serve as the source of the airstream. When we speak, the airstream flows from the lungs to pass through the larynx. The speech sound is modified by the glottis through the vocal cords.

When the vocal cords come together they narrow the glottis through which the airstream flows and the flow of the air makes the vocal cords vibrate. Speech sounds produced when the vocal cords are vibrating is called "voiced sounds". When the vocal cords are drawn apart, there is no vibration and the sounds produced are called voiceless sounds.

All the vowel sounds are voiced. But a consonant may be voiced or voiceless depending on the state of the glottis.

Diagram Showing English Vowel Chart

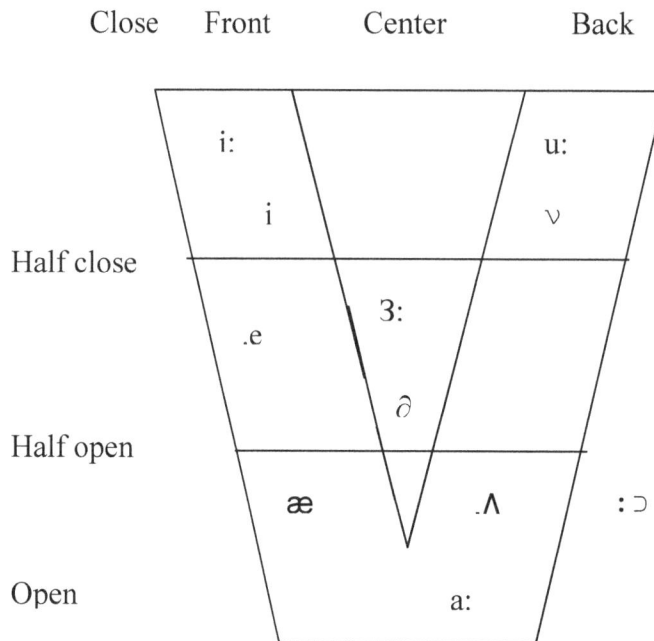

Close   Front   Center   Back

```
                 i:                    u:

                  i                     ʋ

Half close ─────────────────────────────────
                          3:
               .e
                           ∂

Half open  ─────────────────────────────────
                  æ            .ʌ        : ɔ

Open                          a:
```

Further up the throat, the air passage bifurcates to create two channels through which the air stream can pass. One of the channels leads to the oral cavity (mouth) and the other to the nasal cavity (nose). The second modification after the vocal cords is the velum. The velum can be raised to cover the channel that leads into the nasal cavity in order to allow the air stream to flow through the mouth for the production of oral sounds or the velum may be lowered to block the channel that leads into the oral cavity so the air stream flows through the nose for the production of nasal sounds.

In English language we have the following Alphabets:-

A B C D E F G H I J K L M N O P Q R S T U V W X Y Z-
IN CAPITAL LETTERS.

IN SMALL LETTER-
A b c d e f g h I j k l m n o p q r s t u v w x y z.

The next organs of phonation are oral or mouth organs. The hard palate: the teeth ridge: (alveolar ridge) the tongue which is divided into the front, central and back parts, the lips and teeth.

The tongue is so important in speech production that language is synonymous to tongue. The tongue can assume different shapes and positions and these positions and shapes give vowel sounds their distinguish qualities.

VOWELS:

Speech sounds are divisible into the categories, vowel sounds and consonant sounds. There are forty-four sounds segments in both vowels and consonants; twenty of them being vowel sound. However, it should be noted that the vowels are sustainable vocal sounds made without audible stopping of breath of friction in the passage out through the mouth letters or symbols used are /a e i o u/ the symbols are i; I, e, /, a:, D, V, u:, , ≥ : ∝/

The production of vowels takes place as the airstream flows from the lungs to the mouth without any obstruction.

The vowels in English are classified into pure vowels (monothongs) and dipthongs. There are 12 pure vowels and 8 dipthongs.

VOWELS IN ENGLISH

1. /I:/ as in peace; seat; field .

2. /I/ as in Monday; Sit pretty, filled.

3. /ɛ/ as in Ten; bury; jealous, ate.

4. /a/ as in cat, fan, sacks, sang

5. /a:/ as in arm, psalm, part, alms.

6. /ɔ/ as in pot, cock, sausage, cough.

7. /ɔ:/ as in port, cork, dawn, stalk.

8. /v/ as in put, books, should, pull.

11

9. /u:/ as in stool, boots, two, pool.

10. /ʌ/as in blood, cup, cut, such.

11. /3:/as in firm, first, journey, shirt.

12./ə/ as in was, some, ago.

13. /ei/ as in page, late, day, wage.

14. /ai/ As in five, die, why, child.

15. /ɔ:/ as in boy, coy, joy, employ.

16. /əʊ/ as in home, bone, snow, load.

17. /aʊ/ as in now, house, louse, cow.

18. /īə/ as in near, wear, fear, gear.

19. /3ə/ as in air, rare, fair, pair.

20. /ʊə / as in tour, pure, poor.

NOTE: For this exercise the use of a pronouncing dictionary or an advanced learner's dictionary will be of a great help.

NOTE: That there are 5 long vowels and 7 short vowels.

CONSONANTS

There are 24 English consonant sounds. A consonant is different from a vowel in that is a speech sound produced with the obstruction of the airstream. The obstruction may be "partial" or "total". Consonants are described in terms of place of articulation, manner of articulation and the state of the glottis.

1. /p/ voiceless, bilabial plosive as in pop, tap.

2. /b/ voiced bilabial plosive as in bad, rubber.

3. /t/ voiceless Alveolar plosive as in tea, set.

4. /d/ voiceless alveolar plosive as in dip, hide.

5. /k/ voiceless velar plosive as in come, black.

6. /g/ voiced velar plosive as in got, target.

7. /f/ voiceless labio-dental fricative in fan, ferry.

8. /v/ voiced labio-dental fricative in van, very.

9. /Θ/ voiced dental fricative as in think, both.

10. / δ/ Voiced dental fricative as in this, father.

11. /ʃ/ voiceless palato-alveolar fricative, she, chair.

12. /3/ voiced palato-alveolar as in vision, measure.

13. /s/ voiceless alveolar fricative as in sip, place.

14. /z/ voiced alveolar fricative as in sizes, razor.

15. /h/ voiceless glottal fricative as in hat, behave.

16. /ts/ voiceless palato-alveolar, alveolar affricate rich, chin.

17.   /d3/ voiced palato-alveolar affricate as in page, June.

18.   /l/ alveolar lateral as in lock, sell.

19.   /r/ alveolar liquid as in rope, borrow.

20.   /w/ bilabial approximate (semi-vowel) as in win, sweet.

21.   /j/ palatal approximate (semi-vowel) as in you, are.

22.   /m/ bilabial nasal as in man, him.

23.   /n/ alveolar nasal as in no, rain

24.   /ŋ/ velar nasal as in sing, finger.

FURTHER ORAL ENGLISH

A DISTINCTION BETWEEN THE PURE VOWELS, DIPTHONGS AND CONSONANTS

PURE VOWELS

1. I: as in feat

2. I as in fit

3. e as in pet

4. a as in pack

5. a: as in park

6. as in pot ɒ

7. ɔ: as in born

8. ʊ as in put

9. Y: as in spoon

10.   ʌ as in cup

11.   3 as in bird

12.   ∂ as in above

DIPTHONGS

1. ei as in may

2. ∂u as in home

3. ai as in mine

4. au as in bow

5. ɔi as in toil

6. lə as in peer

7. eə as in pear

8. uə as in tour

CONSONANTS

1. P as in plant

2. t as in ten

3. k as in come

4. b as in band

5. d as in dance

6. g as in game

7. f as in four

8. v as in van

9. θ as in thank

10. d as in that

11. s as in same

12. z as in zeal

13. S as in sharp

14. 3 as in measure

15. m as in main

16. n as in name

17. D as in long

18.	(a) as in lame

Nevertheless, it should be noted by the student that, there are no conventional names for these symbols. Although, it is recommended that every teacher adopts a method of naming them, that is, with regard to the vowels, it is recommended that they be designated by their number e.g. /d/ can be called vowel No.4 and /3i/ vowel No.11.

In the same way, Dipthong No.14 stands for / ∂u/ and Dipthong No.19 for /ed/.

For consonants, one can easily speak of 'the dee sound' (for d), 'the ef-sound (for f), 'the 10-sound, (for θ), 'the dl:- sound (for d), 'the Iʃ-sound (for ʃ), 'the 3i-sound for {3} etc

DIAGRAM OF A VOWEL CHART

The following diagram is meant to give you a cursory view of the points of articulations in both vowel, and consonants words.

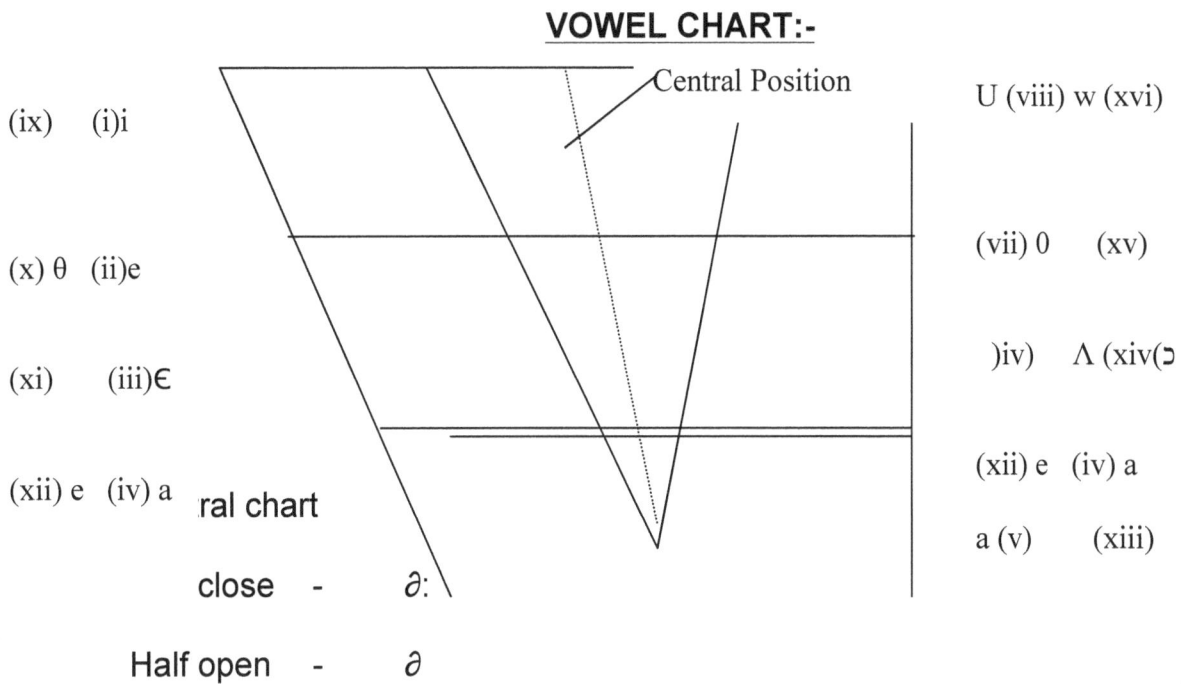

VOWEL CHART:-

(ix)   (i)i

(x) θ (ii)e

(xi)   (iii)∈

(xii) e (iv) a

ral chart

close   -   ∂:

Half open   -   ∂

Central Position

U (viii) w (xvi)

(vii) 0   (xv)

)iv)   Λ (xiv(ɔ

(xii) e (iv) a

a (v)   (xiii)

NOW LET TREAT THE VOWEL CONTRASTS /i:/ and /i/

VOWEL (3)

(A)	/i:/	/I/	(B)
	week	wick	
	feel	fill	
	bead	bid	
	green	grin	
	ease	is	
	sheep	ship	
	each	itch	

18

peel	pill
seat	sit
sleep	slip
leak	lick
heap	hip
wheat	wit
been	bin
feet	fit
leave	live
beat	bit
deed	did

WORD CONSONANT VOWELS /e/ and /I/

/e/	/I/
gem	jam
shell	shall
bend	band
pet	pat
beg	bag
peck	pack
said	sad
lend	land
leg	lag
text	taxed
send	sand

/ɒ/	/ɔ:/
swan	sworn
cot	court
rot	wrought
nock	hawk
cod	cord
what	wart
don	dawn
hod	hoard
knotty	naughty

VOWEL WORD CONTRAST /iə/ and /eə/

(A) /Iə/ /iə/	(B) /eə/
dear	dare
sheer	share
ear	air
tier	tare
here	hare
peer	pear
fear	fair

beer	bare
cheer	chair
sneer	snare
steer	stair
mere	mayor
lear	lair
spear	spare

VOWEL CONTRAST /ʃ/ and /ʌ/

(A) /ʃ/	and /ʌ/
lack	luck
dam	dumb
track	truck
bade	bud
gnat	nut

/ɒ/	/ʌ/
fan	fun
snag	snug
tack	tuck

ram	run
camp	dump
bat	butt
cat	cut
lag	lug
pan	pun
rash	rush
rabble	rubble

VOWEL WORD CONTRAST /D/ AND /ʌ/

/D/	/ʌ/
cot	cut
song	sung
gone	gun
hot	hut
cop	cup
long	lung
lock	luck
doll	dull
not	nut
box	bucks
cough	cuff

shot	shut
boss	bus
rob	rub
corpse	cups
fond	fund
mosque	musk

SENTENCES FOR PRACTICE

1) The Don with the cuffs often wonders about the hog near the hut.

2) He shot the luckless dog in the hut with his gun

3) The donkey and the monkey are fond of wandering near the hut.

4) His boss who was traveling on the bus did not eat the salad.

/e/	/D/
ten	tan
bet	bat
set	sat
mess	mass
met	mat
pen	pan
quess	gas
hen	ham
bed	bad

VOWEL WORD CONTRAST /ɪ/ and /a:/

(A) /ɪ/	(B) /a:/
cat	cart
match	march
stack	stark
pat	part
chat	chart
lack	lark
hat	heart
back	bark
badge	barge
have	halve
hath	hearth

SENTENCES FOR PRACTICE

1) That dog always barks at people when they give him their back.

2) The football match will take place in March.

3) Mark, pack your clothes before you go to the park.

4) John chartered the taxi and started to chat with the driver.

5) The ant got into my aunt's armpit.

(A) /ɒ/	/ɔː/ (B)
wad	ward
not	nought
stock	storck
pot	port
god	gored
spot	sport
cock	cork
shot	short
fox	forks

CONSONANT CHART

SOUND	BILABIAL	LABIO-DENTAL	INTER-DENTAL	ALVEOLAR	PALATAL	PALATO-ALVEOLAR	VELAR	UVULAR	GLOTAL	LABIO-VELAR
	b			d	d		g			Gb
		P		t	c		k		٦	Kp
VIOCED PLOSIVE VOICELESS		B	v		z	J	3	r	t	
	Φ	F	θ	s		ʃ	X		h	
VD FRICATEVES VL			0			d₃				
						ts				
VD AFFRICATE VL	M			ת	ת		מ			
					ת		מ			
VD NASAL VL					!					
					!					
VD LATERAL VL				r						
VD GLIDE VL										

V.D.	=	VIOCED	
V.L.	=	VOICELESS	

CONSONANTS

Consonant words contrasts /p/ and /b/; /t/ and /d/

/p/	/b/	/t/	/d/
part	bark	bat	bad
pet	bet	kilt	killed
pig	big	bent	bend
		height	hide
petty	betty	tie	die
apportion	abortion	sat	sad
rapid	rabid	wrote	rode
		bit	bid
nipple	bibble	but	bud
staple	stable	truck	duck
repel	rebel	metal	medal
crumple	crumble	water	wander
lapel	label	latter	ladder
mopping	mobbing	written	ridden
sopping	sobbing	putting	pudding
maple	mabel	betting	bedding

SENTENCES FOR PRACTICE

1) I bet you that label will soon crumble under Mabel's care.
2) While Betty was trying to repel the big pig, pretty Kehinde was sobbing.
3) When you go to the park, the dog will surely bark and rip off your cloths.
4) She rebelled against the idea of marrying a man with big nipples

SENTENCES FOR PRACTICE

1) As Jim was sad he sat and wrote a bit of poetry.
2) Your height makes it impossible for you to hide in that corner.
3) The warder brought water and bedding for the prisoners.
4) The moment they tied him like a thief he began to confess immediately.
5) He has written about horses but has never ridden one himself.

It should be noted that certain consonantal words like 'p' and "b" are not sounded in the following words. For instance,

(1) psalm, (2) receipt (3) lamb (4) psychology (5) doubt (6) womb (7) pheumonia (8) climb (9) cupboard (10) plumber (11) debt (12) tomb (13) coup (14) debtor (15) psychiatry (16) psyche (17) comb (18) bomb (19) bomber (20) dumb (21) subtle (22) thumb (23) numb.

Also consonants /t/ and /d/ are not sounded in some expressions like: (1)castle (2) Christmas (3) fasten (4) ballet (5) often (6) bouquet (7) hasten (8) depot (9) Windsor (10) nestle (11) listen (12) gristle (13) handsome (14)thistle (15) bristle (16)chestnut (17) Wednesday (19)handkerchief (20)wrestle.

CONSONANT CONTRAST /k/ and /g/

/k/	/g/
leak	league
pick	pig
come	gum
coal	goal
crate	great
clock	clog
rack	rag
pluck	plug
kilt	guilt
card	guard
lock	log
ankle	angle
decree	degree
lacking	lagging
biker	bigger

SYLLABIC PATTERN IN ENGLISH

When we speak, we produce vowels and consonants which are individual (segmental) contrastive sound units of the language. Since speech is a continuous activity, the speaker produces a chain of vowels and consonants which may combine to form a larger units called a **SYLLABLE.**

Two or more syllables may also combine to form a larger unit called word.

In actual speech process, a speaker puts the vowels and consonants together to form words like 'rig', 'trip', imput, "giver" and a number of other words. Most of these words contain one syllable and are therefore, called "MONOSYLLABIC WORDS". But each of the word 'imput' 'giver' has two syllables.

The two syllables in imput are separated with a dash in-put, while giver is also separated into two syllables gi-ver. From this illustration, we can see that speech sounds combine to form syllables while syllables may combine to form words.

Sometimes, however, a single sound unit usually a vowel, may serve both as a syllable and a word.

The word "are" for instance is just a vowel pronounced /a:/. This word functions as a vowel and a syllable.

However, the sounds of the English language combine to form syllables or words, these sounds are arranged in such a way that they will form an acceptable sequences.

From the set of sounds already mentioned a sequence like pit or tip can be formed but the language does not permit a sequence like tpi or pti. The arrangement (patterning of speech sounds) into acceptable sequences in a syllable gives rise to what is called syllabic structure.

An English syllable may have three parts namely- onset, peak, closure. The peak is obligatory, from the onset or the closure may be absent.

Study these examples:-

i)   get   =   gΣt   (g - Σ - t)

ii)   beat =   bi:t   (b-i: -t)

iii)   league   =   li:g   (l – i: - g)

iv)   food =   fu:d   (f- u: - d)

v)   do   =   du: (d-u:)

A vowel is usually the peak of a syllable and, it is called the peak because, it is the most important part of the syllable.

Each of the words under column A is a monosyllabic word, which has either /l/ or /n/ as the final consonant. In this word a vowel functions as the PEAK or NUCLEUS. On the other hand, each of the words under column B has two syllables.

The first syllable in each case has a vowel as the peak but the last syllable has no vowel. In those syllable without a vowel /l̩/ or /n/ functions as the peak/nucleus.

When we look at the written form, some of these syllables seem to contain vowels; in actual pronunciation there is no vowel. The transcribed form shows the correct pronunciation.

From more practice, consult a pronunciation dictionary, when you are not sure of the correct pronunciation of any word.

STRESS

(Segmental features and suprasegmental features)

The vowels and consonants are speech sounds which can be identified and described as discrete segments with individual phonetic features. The word pit is made up of 3 sound- units with each phonetic feature.

There are features of speech which cannot be broken into individual units like the vowels and consonant. These features are STRESS, RHYTHM (Pitch) and INTONATION.

They are called SUPRASEGMENTAL FEATURES because they function within larger units like words, phrases and sentences. They are so important in speech that they do not only affect the quality of the vowel but also affect our message when we speak e.g. stress is an important feature of speech which creates problem to many non-english speakers of English. As the air stream flows during speech, we exert some equal effort for the production of all sounds, because some syllables are uttered with greater breath effort and muscular energy than the others. Such syllables which are uttered with greater muscular energy are louder and longer and are therefore said to be "STRESSED'.

FEATURES OF A STRESSED SYLLABLE

1) A stressed syllable is longer than the unstressed syllable.

   <u>HOSTLE</u>

2) It is uttered with greater energy than the unstressed.

3) It has a higher pitch of the voice than the unstressed.

There are 3 degrees of stress in English. Primary, secondary and unstressed, but for the purpose of this study, we shall recognize only 2- stressed and unstressed. A stressed syllable is indicated by placing a stroke at the beginning of the syllable as in 'female or behind.

1) Any word in English said in isolation must be stressed.

2) Any word in English of more than one syllable usually carries a stress in one of its syllables e.g.

1. Hos-tel	9. Con-tain
2. Ea-ting	10. Un-less
3. Cov-er	11. Pre-tend
	12. Un-known
4. Pill-ow	13. Un-til
5. Ne-ver	14. Re-main
	15. ex-ceed
6. Ta-ble	16. be-hind
7. Win-dow	17. can-teen

If a word consists of two syllables, the first syllable is usually stressed, if the first syllable is a prefix, the second attracts the stress while the first syllable is unstressed. See example above.

Stress has meaning in English. A change in the stress pattern of a word in English may change its meaning. A word which is used as a noun in one sentence with stress on the first syllable may become a verb in another sentence if the stress is shifted to the second syllable.

NOUN	**VERB**
OBject	obJECT
CONtest	conTEST
CONvict	conVICT
TRANSport	transPORT
REbel	reBEL
CONtrast	conTRAST
PROtest	proTEST
EScort	esCORT
REcord	reCORD
IMport	imPORT

ADJECTIVE	**VERB**
PREsent	preSENT
PERfect	perFECT

Words of 3 Syllables

(1) DElicate   (ii) discussion   (iii) disaGREE

(iv) BAchelor   (v) draMAtic   (vi) underSTAND

(vii) QUANtity   (viii) OCCAsion   (ix) afterNOON

SENTENCE STRESS

The importance of stress in conveying the appropriate meaning or information is shown as in the following examples:-

(a)   I saw John (, not some other person)

(b)   I saw John (saw, not heard of him).

(c)   I saw John (not James).

(d)   May I borrow your pen? (not hire or steal it).

(e)   My I borrow your pen? (not your pencil).

INTONATION

Intonation is very important in spoken English. When one discusses in English, the meaning of an utterance is not only affected by the stress but also by the pitch of voice.

- Intonation: This means that the stress and intonation work together to give special meaning and emphasis to an utterance. Intonation in English show the attitude of the speaker in English.

- Rising and Falling patterns: The rising and falling pitch (intonation) indicates whether a sentence is a:

(i) Statement

(ii) Command

(iii) Question or exclamation.

EXAMPLES:-

1. Statement or giving information carries a falling tune e.g.

   They came to the <u>factory</u> collected their <u>goods,</u> and went

   <u>way.</u>

   Fall, fall, fall (tune).

2. Question that demands yes or no takes a rising tune e.g.

   Did you remove the chair? He asked politely.

   (followed by a rising tag).

3. Get out of my house! He cried angrily

   (tune followed by low-level tag).

STATEMENT

A. John works hard in school

B. <u>COMMAND</u>

   Stand under the tree

   Don't disobey your teachers.

C. <u>WH-QUESTION</u>

Why are you late?

How did you handle the case?

EXCLAMATION

What a good result! ↘

How pretty she looks! ↘

Is the wine sweet? ↘

Will Monday be good for it? ↗

www.ingramcontent.com/pod-product-compliance
Lightning Source LLC
Chambersburg PA
CBHW081601040426
42448CB00013B/3152

9780956941565